Nigel Dennis

KRUGER

Text by Michael Brett

Nigel Dennis

KRUGER

Text by Michael Brett

Struik Publishers
(a division of New Holland Publishing (South Africa) (Pty) Ltd)
Cornelis Struik House, 80 McKenzie Street, Cape Town 8001
www.struik.co.za

New Holland Publishing is a member of the Johnnic Publishing Group.
Log on to our photographic website **www.imagesofafrica.co.za** for an African experience.

First published 2000
3 5 7 9 10 8 6 4 2

Publishing manager: Pippa Parker • Managing editor: Simon Pooley • Designer: Dominic Robson and
Beverley Dodd • Cartographer: Michael Brett • Proofreader: Brenda Brickman

Reproduction by Hirt and Carter Cape (Pty) Ltd
Printed and bound by Kyodo Printing Co (Singapore) (Pte) Ltd, Singapore

ISBN 1 86872 421 2

Front cover A hunting lioness is a portrait of unwavering vigilance and supreme prowess.
Back cover A ground hornbill holding an egg in its bill; this is probably a form of dominance behaviour.
Frontispiece A young chacma baboon. *Previous page* The northern Kruger bushveld is noted for its huge
baobabs. Some specimens are thought to be as much as 1 500 years old. *Opposite* A cheetah hunting.

Acknowledgements

I wish to thank South African National Parks for their generous assistance and permission to photograph
in the Kruger National Park. My photography was conducted under the guidance of SANP. Sincere thanks
to all the Kruger staff, with special thanks to the following: Johan van Graan, Hein Grobler, Andy and Delise
Hagget, David Mabunda, Marc and Sue McDonald, Gus Mills, Flip Nel, Angus Rabie, Schalk and Lorretha van
der Sandt, Mbongani Thukela, Steve Whitfield and Antoinette van Wyk. Whilst the great majority of
photography was undertaken in the Kruger National Park itself, I also spent time in the adjoining Sabi
Sand Reserve. I am most grateful to Sharon Joss and Warren Green of Sabi Sabi for their kindness and
generosity. As always my biggest thank you must go to my wife Wendy, for her companionship on all our
visits to the Park.
                                                                                    Nigel Dennis

Vegetation zones for the map of Kruger are based on research conducted by Willem Gertenbach.

References

Braack, L.E.O. (1996) *Globetrotter Travel Guide – Kruger National Park*. New Holland, London, Cape Town;
Carruthers, J. (1995) *The Kruger National Park – A Social and Political History*. University of Natal Press,
Pietermaritzburg; Dennis, N. J. and Scoles, R. J. (1995) *The Kruger National Park – Wonders of an African Eden*.
New Holland, London, Cape Town; Sinclair, I. and White, I. (1991) *Field Guide to the Birds of the Kruger
National Park*. Struik, Cape Town; Smuts, G.L. (1982) *Lion*. Macmillan, Johannesburg; Stevenson-Hamilton,
J. (1993 – reprint) *South African Eden – The Kruger National Park 1902-1946*. Struik, Cape Town.

INTRODUCTION

A long ripple in the earth's crust, the Escarpment is a conspicuous landmark along the eastern edge of South Africa, separating the temperate grasslands of the Highveld from the sun-baked savannas of the Lowveld. The Escarpment's elevated, grassy summit is often mist shrouded; streams tumble down rocky stairways that give way to waterfalls, and dense forests spread across the valleys like shadows. From the cool summit, the view to the east is across a seemingly endless landscape of mauve-grey bush, punctuated occasionally by low hills and rocky outcrops. In some places, the great sweep of this vast plain is interrupted by rivers carving verdant corridors across the dry land. Fed by rain falling on the Escarpment, these perennial rivers transform this immense, semi-arid wilderness of dry woodland and savanna, and sustain a great abundance of plants, insects, reptiles, birds and mammals.

Across these unbounded, bush-covered expanses everything is constantly changing: centuries-old trees are struck by lightning and are reduced to a small pile of ash; vegetation communities are altered as plants are influenced by drought, fire and animals; and fluctuations in animal populations closely track climatic change. And yet the cycle of life – birth, childhood, maturity, old age and death – ensures that things remain essentially the same. Viewed against the complexity and enormity of the entire system, minor changes and events are easily blurred. Individual lives and events are obscured by summer's new growth, washed away by thunderstorms and covered over by the ceaseless procession of time.

In the heart of the Lowveld, stretching for 352 kilometres from north to south along the Mozambique border, one of the world's foremost national parks can be found. This is the Kruger National Park, a wildlife sanctuary larger in area than Israel. Covering 19 624 square kilometres and averaging 60 kilometres in width, Kruger provides a refuge for 147 mammal species, 500 species of birds, 116 reptiles, 34 amphibians, 49 fishes, 457 types of trees and shrubs, 1 500 smaller plants, and countless insects.

Each year approximately 950 000 people visit the Kruger Park, and half of them stay overnight in the 26 rest camps that range from the intimate 19-bed Malelane, bordering the Crocodile River in the extreme south, to historic Punda Maria in the far north. South Africans account for 80 per cent of all visitors, and for many a visit to Kruger has become a kind of spiritual pilgrimage. An entire subculture of devotees has developed over the past 70 years around the unpredictability of wildlife viewing, the apparent endlessness of the wilderness and the Park's unique atmosphere. And it is these ardent supporters who are the Park's greatest defenders. Kruger epitomises for many the rejuvenating and healing qualities of Nature, allowing its visitors to escape the increasing pressures of modern urban life and the Information Age.

The Park's rest camps are connected by a 2 600-kilometre network of all-weather roads, which allow visitors to explore its diverse habitats on their own and without the need to hire a guide. Income from tourism and trading activities generates more than R200-million per year, and the Kruger Park plays a major role in the Lowveld's economy. Purely in terms of facilities and the range of accommodation offered, no national park anywhere in the world can match what Kruger has to offer. Even the most popular national parks in the United States cannot equal the number of rest camps and the extent of the road network. This fact alludes to an apparent contradiction: South Africa's largest wildlife reserve and one of its most unspoilt wildernesses is at the same time one of the most developed and accessible ecotourism destinations in the country.

Above Nkumbe lookout offers superb views across Kruger.
Opposite Impala are Kruger's most abundant antelope species.

THE PAST

The Lowveld plains have been traversed by a host of travellers in search of fortune, but few memorials indicate their paths or recall their endeavours. A clump of tall marula trees, a colossal baobab, a patch of ash – all are silent witnesses to the many explorers who have passed by in search of gold, ivory, trophies and adventure. Likewise, while Kruger appears to be an unspoiled relic of a formerly vast wilderness, and still retains many of the natural ecological forces that governed the region in the past, the Park is also very much the product of the historical events that took place in South Africa during the nineteenth and twentieth centuries. In order to comprehend how much of the present was fashioned by the past, it is necessary to delve into history and trace the human pathways that have intersected and merged together to produce one of the world's foremost wildlife sanctuaries.

From Thulamela to the Trekkers

At the beginning of the fifteenth century the Rozvi Kingdom centred on Great Zimbabwe splintered into several fragments. One offshoot migrated south across the Limpopo and built a stone-walled citadel on the cliffs overlooking the east bank of the Luvuvhu River, in what is now the northernmost corner of Kruger. At the entrance, on the hill summit, the King's personal guards would escort visitors into the stone-walled enclosure where skilled artisans fashioned gold necklaces, beads and bracelets. Together with ivory these ornaments were exchanged for commodities such as glass beads from India, porcelain from China and iron gongs from West Africa. Thulamela shows that there were highly advanced indigenous settlements in the Lowveld centuries before the area was first explored by European hunters and later settled by missionaries, traders and miners.

For a variety of reasons, the indigenous peoples had a limited impact on wildlife numbers. Although there is evidence that ivory was a major trade item, and trade with Arab and Asian lands can be traced back many centuries, the amount of ivory consumed did not pose a significant threat to the elephant population.

When Europeans began arriving in the Cape from 1652, however, they viewed wildlife as an abundant and limitless resource, and rapidly set about exterminating it with the aid of firearms. By 1800, elephant, buffalo, rhino, hippo and lion were all extinct in the settled regions of the Cape.

In the 1830s many Afrikaners trekked away from the Cape, and established independent republics. North of the Vaal River, the settlers created several rival republics, but by 1860 they were consolidated into the *Zuid-Afrikaansche Republiek* (ZAR), a 300 000-square-kilometre territory stretching from the Vaal River to the Limpopo River. The economy of the new republic depended on the exploitation of wildlife, in particular elephant, and it was not long before big game was exterminated on the more hospitable, plateau regions.

The First Wildlife Sanctuaries

Like lightning striking iron-rich hills, the crack of gunfire soon reverberated across the quiet valleys of the Lowveld. The discovery of gold in 1871, near Sabie, brought many fortune-seekers to the area and hastened the demise of wildlife. When Percy FitzPatrick drove his wagons through the region in 1885, big game had already disappeared from the Lowveld, and there is no mention in his famous book – *Jock of the Bushveld* – of elephant, rhino, hippo, giraffe or eland.

On the road between Pretoriuskop and Afsaal, plaques mark the route followed by Percy FitzPatrick, and his dog Jock, in 1885.

At Paul Kruger Gate this granite statue commemorates the president of the ZAR.

A simple bronze plaque on the imposing Shirimantanga Koppie – Stevenson-Hamilton's favourite retreat – honours the man who devoted 44 years to the development of the Park.

Although there was growing concern over the rapid destruction of wildlife in the ZAR, the government was slow to respond. The establishment of game sanctuaries was first debated in the *Volksraad* (People's Council) in August 1889, but it took five years before the first game reserve was gazetted on 13 June 1894. This reserve, a 175-square-kilometre corridor comprising seven farms in the extreme southeastern corner of the ZAR, arguably represented the first serious attempt to protect wildlife on the African continent, and a major portion of the original sanctuary has survived to the present day.

Four other reserves were proclaimed in the ZAR before the nucleus of the Kruger Park, the Sabi Game Reserve, was established. Several members of the Volksraad were in favour of setting aside a large area in the Lowveld, but the ZAR government appeared to be in no hurry and un-controlled hunting persisted. Representatives Loveday and Van Wijk introduced a motion in September 1895 compelling the government to act, but no progress was made until Loveday again raised the matter two years later. Eventually, a proclamation signed by President Paul Kruger was published on 26 March 1898 establishing the Sabi Game Reserve.

This game reserve, a 4 600-square-kilometre wedge of land bordered by the Crocodile and Sabie rivers, was the largest of the reserves established by the ZAR. It had taken nearly nine years from President Kruger's speech in the Volksraad, in which he proposed setting aside reserves throughout the republic, to the date of proclamation. The post of Warden was created later in the year, but progress in developing the reserve was soon halted by the outbreak of the Anglo-Boer War on 11 October 1899.

When the war ended in May 1902, Milner's caretaker government in Pretoria reproclaimed three of the ZAR's reserves. In July 1902, James Stevenson-Hamilton was appointed Warden of the re-established Sabi Game Reserve. After hiring four assistants, and acquiring three ponies and a single wagon drawn by six oxen, he entered the reserve on 6 August 1902 and trekked in an easterly direction from Pretoriuskop. He was initially disappointed by an apparent absence of game and wrote, 'Indeed it was not until the fourth day, our progress having been delayed by a broken *disselboom* [wagon shaft], that we came across a few tracks of zebra, waterbuck and impala. The following morning I saw, in the flesh, a reedbuck ewe, a duiker and two jackal and in the evening was much heartened by the appearance of a herd of nearly thirty impala.'

With the military discipline that he had acquired at Sand-hurst, and while serving as an officer in the 6th Inniskilling Dragoons in Natal, Stevenson-Hamilton devoted his energies to his newly-chosen career and within a year he convinced his superiors in Pretoria of the need to triple the size of the Sabi Reserve. In the same year the Singwitsi Game Reserve, incorporating 9 000 square kilometres of land between the Letaba and Luvuvhu rivers, was proclaimed. Although Stevenson-Hamilton had not been involved in this proclamation, he was delighted at the news and appointed Major Fraser, a fellow Scot, as Warden of Singwitsi. Stevenson-Hamilton was now in command of an immense 22 000 square kilometres of untamed bushveld.

EARLY PRESERVATIONISTS

Schooled in Victorian etiquette and military discipline, early Park rangers were revolted by the wanton destruction of much of South Africa's wildlife that had occurred in the nineteenth century. In response to this mass eradication, a preservationist backlash sought to restore the surviving relic herds to levels where sustainable utilisation by sport hunters would again be possible. So, many early rangers viewed the job of a nature conservator primarily as a protector of antelope and 'game animals', in the same way as the Medieval gamekeeper protected the royal deer from enemies both human and animal. (In America, where this philosophy was also prevalent at the time, wolves were hunted to extinction in Yellowstone National Park.)

In the Sabi Game Reserve, justification for controlling predators was based on the argument that hoofed animals had been severely depleted during the Anglo-Boer War and were in danger of extinction, while predators were regarded as overabundant and a direct threat to the survival of antelope. Stevenson-Hamilton, however, was not in favour of eradicating predators from the reserve, and instead adopted a policy of reducing them to lower levels until game populations increased. He also faced constant pressure from neighbouring landowners and hunting associations to eliminate predators as they were seen as posing a threat to both livestock and game.

In 1902 Stevenson-Hamilton estimated that the Sabi Game Reserve contained a relic 5 giraffe, 5 tsessebe, 8 buffalo, 12 sable, 15 hippo, 35 kudu, 40 blue wildebeest, 100 waterbuck and large numbers of impala, reedbuck, steenbok and grey duiker. A decade later he was able to report that the Sabi and Singwitsi reserves together sustained 25 elephant, 200 hippo, 250 giraffe, 250 buffalo, 1 500 sable, 3 000 zebra, 4 500 blue wildebeest, 1 000 tsessebe, 1 500 kudu, 6 000 waterbuck and 7 000 impala. In 1912 he presented a plan to the British Colonial Secretary, Sir Patrick Duncan, and General Jan Smuts, Minister of Finance, Interior and Defence, recommending that the two consolidated reserves should be declared a national park.

As antelope numbers increased, so predators increased proportionately. Stevenson-Hamilton had already begun to view predators as an important component of the ecosystem, but predator control programmes were still carried out and up to 1927 a total of 1 272 lion, 660 leopard, 269 cheetah, 521 hyaena and 1 142 wild dog were culled. Rangers also shot 2 006 baboons, 635 crocodiles, 1 363 poisonous snakes, 558 eagles and many smaller predators. An interesting statistic is the number of cheetah and wild dog that were shot. In both instances the present population of these endangered predators is considerably less than the number culled. It seems that the early control schemes, and subsequent management policies such as the provision of artificial water holes, tipped the balance in favour of lions at the expense of other predators.

Early rangers regarded the exquisite leopard as a threat to game.

CONSERVATION REPLACES PRESERVATION

Early in his career Stevenson-Hamilton had shown evidence that he was moving away from a preservationist approach to a more holistic conservation ethic, as evidenced in his belief in 'the balance of Nature', where every species enjoys its rightful place. Not only did this guarantee all species a vital role in the ecosystem, but he was able to deflect attempts to have the reserve thrown open to the English sportsmen who dominated the wildlife preservation associations of the day.

At the same time, he began to develop the notion that 'the ideal should be to show the country and the animals in it to the public as God made both.'

In May 1926 his tireless dedication to the cause of nature conservation was rewarded, and the South African Parliament passed an act establishing the Kruger National Park. The following year only three cars visited the Park and revenue from tourism amounted to a paltry £3. But by 1928 visitor traffic had increased to 850 people in 180 cars, and by the end of 1929 a total of 78 thatched huts had been completed in eight rest camps. Viewing wild animals *in the wild* was a new experience for the urban residents of South Africa, who undertook the often eventful journey to the Lowveld along rutted dirt roads that negotiated rocky passes and flooded river crossings. It soon became apparent that the animal visitors were most interested in seeing was the lion, followed by giraffe and elephant.

Stevenson-Hamilton retired in 1946 after serving as Warden for 44 years. By this time the Kruger Park had grown into a popular tourist destination and 10 000 cars now passed through its gates each year. Tourist facilities had been greatly expanded since 1927, and 13 rest camps had been constructed. Colonel Sandenbergh, a South African Air Force officer, succeeded Stevenson-Hamilton. His appointment coincided with a severe drought and a 'Water for Game' fund was launched, which raised money for drilling 46 boreholes. Lions remained the principal drawcard and the Lower Sabie road consistently offered the best sightings. But in 1949 Sandenbergh re-instated the predator control programme, arguing that predators were living off the 'capital' and not on surplus game as Nature had intended.

When Sandenbergh resigned in 1953, Senior Ranger Steyn became Warden. His appointment coincided with the end of a severe 10-year drought in the Lowveld, and significant declines in sable, roan, tsessebe, waterbuck and reedbuck were noted, all water-dependent species that also require tall grassland. Steyn was concerned, arguing that the Kruger Park owed its existence to predator control programmes, and these controls were therefore essential for maintaining a balance between predators and prey. While public opinion in the 1920s had favoured lion eradication, in the 1950s opinions had undergone a dramatic swing in favour of their protection. To avoid further criticism, it was decided that details of the control programme would be kept secret, and would not be included in the annual reports presented to Parliament. The programme was stepped up and cheetah, leopard and wild dog were also killed. In 1956 a new

Stevenson-Hamilton's belief that lions are an essential ingredient of the Park's ecosystem was not supported by many of his game rangers.

proposal recommended removing 40 per cent of all lions, and it was only after a lengthy presentation by the Park's assistant biologist, Dr U de V Pienaar, that the culling plan was amended two years later.

So, despite Stevenson-Hamilton's early reservations, it was only in 1960 that the last vestiges of the original Victorian 'deer park' philosophy finally disappeared and the regular culling of predators ceased. With the wisdom of hindsight, it appears that arguments for controlling predators were unfounded. No natural system will continue in a state of imbalance indefinitely. A shortage of available prey will soon result in a decline in predators as it becomes increasingly difficult for them to locate food.

A QUESTION OF BALANCE

After a century of dedicated conservation, Kruger Park is currently home to 100 000 impala, 21 000 buffalo, 13 000 wildebeest, 4 000 kudu, smaller populations of 13 other antelope species, 29 000 zebra, 9 000 elephant, 5 500 giraffe, 2 600 white rhino, 2 300 hippo, 1 500 warthog, 2 000 lion, 2 000 spotted hyaena, 1 000 leopard, 360 wild dog and 180 cheetah.

Although the Park safeguards an abundance of wildlife, some regions, especially the northern mopaneveld, are classified as dry savanna where fluctuations in rainfall and wildlife numbers are common. Accurate rainfall records have been kept at Skukuza since 1908, and careful analysis of records indicates wet and dry cycles that last approximately 10 years. Within a 10-year cycle there may be one or two years that deviate from the norm, but the general pattern will indicate either a wet or dry phase. In dry years, despite decades of careful management, declines in certain species can be dramatic. During the drought of 1992/3, buffalo plummeted by 48 per cent, while some species such as kudu, waterbuck, tsessebe, roan and sable had begun to decrease from 1986 onwards. Conversely, the drought had virtually no effect on zebra, wildebeest, giraffe, elephant and white rhino.

While Stevenson-Hamilton believed in 'a balance of Nature', evidence suggests that the natural environment is never in a constant state of equilibrium, and is continuously influenced by weather patterns, fire and fluctuating wildlife populations. Nature is therefore never in a balance, or at least not in the way that humans interpret the term.

In the past the Park's biologists sought to manage the system in such a way that fluctuations in wildlife populations were minimised – however, certain management policies were to have a major impact on some species. Where Stevenson-Hamilton had relied on intuition and experience in managing the Park, the 1950s saw the emergence of a corps of scientists, reliant on scientific methods and statistical analysis, that would dominate the management of the Park for more than 40 years.

Under scientific management it was argued that because the Kruger Park was entirely surrounded by a game-proof fence, constant and careful management was necessary. Not only was the veld burnt at regular intervals, and other fires actively discouraged, but wildlife populations were carefully

monitored by conducting an annual census that took over three months to complete. In 1972, Dr U de V Pienaar wrote, 'the Board is trying, by means of the skillful supply of water and scientific control of grazing, to build up the numbers of all herbivorous animals to an optimum level ... considerable numbers of wildebeest and zebra are being captured in the overpopulated areas of the central district and transferred to the underpopulated areas south of the Sabie River.'

The frequent occurrence of droughts, and the bad press that this generated, was addressed by 'Water for Game' campaigns, which raised substantial sums of money. More than 300 windmills and 65 major dams were constructed, often in areas where no natural water had occurred historically. In the Southern Region alone (see map, third following page), 22 windmills and 11 dams were constructed from 1960–1971. The water provision programmes allowed water-dependent species such as zebra and impala to increase. An increase in zebras alters the nature of grasslands and allows lions to colonise vacant territories, thus contributing to the decline of rare antelope such as sable, roan, reedbuck and tsessebe. These antelope require very specific habitats, inhabiting open woodlands and grasslands in prime condition. In the Central Region, 12 new lion prides have become established since the 1950s in areas where artificial water points were provided.

Because water-dependent species thrived as a result of the water provision programmes, scientists then argued that it was therefore necessary to cull elephant, hippo, buffalo, zebra, wildebeest and impala. A census in 1967 counted 6 586 elephants, and park biologists decided to limit the population to 7 000. Culling of elephant and buffalo commenced in the same year. In time, the necessity for these programmes was questioned as a better understanding of the ecosystem emerged, and eventually all culling campaigns, with the exception of those for elephant, were abandoned.

In recent years park managers have retreated from intensive management, and have begun to rethink some of the direct management policies that were applied in the past. A new fire policy allows fires started by lightning to burn without hindrance, and current thinking does not support culling except where certain habitat thresholds have been exceeded.

Management of an intricate ecosystem requires the compilation of a detailed management plan that allows for public input and has built-in capacity for policy changes. In March 1999 a revised management plan was approved. Central to the plan is a clear Mission Statement which is: 'To maintain biodiversity in all its natural facets and to provide human benefits in keeping with the mission of the South African National Parks in a manner which detracts as little as possible from the wilderness qualities of the Kruger National Park.'

The management plan was compiled from the proceedings of 52 workshops involving important role players. One section contains a new elephant management plan that divides Kruger into six zones. Two botanical zones have been established, where the vegetation determines how the area is managed, and these two zones together cover 15 per cent of the Park. One of these is situated in the southwestern corner of Kruger around Pretoriuskop (see map), extending in a corridor southward to the Malelane Mountains; the other is in the Far North, extending from Punda Maria up to Pafuri. Here elephants will be limited to one animal per 2.86 square kilometres (the average density for the whole Park at the old ceiling of 7 000 elephants). Two high impact zones have been established, covering 40 per cent of the Park. One extends from just south of Tshokwane up to the Crocodile River, and the other extends from west of Satara Camp up to near Mopani Camp. Elephants will not be culled or captured in these high impact zones for the foreseeable future. Finally, there are two low impact zones, one extending from the Olifants River to just south of Tshokwane; and the other from Mopani Camp to the edge of the botanical zone around Punda Maria. The low impact zones cover 45 per cent of the Park, and in these areas elephants will be reduced by seven per cent per year by live capture or culling until certain habitat criteria have been met.

One of the most important new policies relates to water. Many of the 300 artificial water holes will be closed. By limiting the distribution of water, many of the imbalances that led to culling in the past will be corrected and natural migratory patterns will hopefully be restored, which benefits the ecosystem by providing long rest periods for the vegetation.

As part of a new move to minimise human interference, six elephant management zones have been proposed for Kruger.

KRUGER BY REGION

For ease of reference, the Kruger National Park is divided into four regions in this book (see map). The 'Southern Region' extends northwards from the southernmost border of the Park as far north as the Sabie River; the 'Central Region' from the Sabie River to the Olifants River; the 'Northern Region' from the Olifants to just south of Punda Maria; and the 'Far North' from Punda Maria up through Pafuri to the Limpopo River. Note that these regions and the names given to them here are not officially recognised.

THE SOUTHERN REGION:
KRUGER'S HISTORIC HEART

Kruger's historic Southern Region is bordered by the Crocodile River in the south and the Sabie River in the north. In the east, along the border with Mozambique, the Lebombo form a rugged ridge of rhyolite. Altitude varies from 140 metres in the east to 600 metres around Pretoriuskop in the west. In the southwestern corner near Berg-en-dal Camp, Khandzalive, the highest point in the Park, rises to 839 metres. In its sheltered valleys specimens of trees which are rare elsewhere in Kruger, such as Cape chestnut (*Calodendrum capense*), white pear (*Apodytes dimidiata*), coral tree (*Erythrina lysistemon*), lavender fever-berry (*Croton gratissimus*) and mountain seringa (*Kirkia wilmsii*) can be found.

Granite underlies more than 80 per cent of the Southern Region and produces the characteristic rounded koppies such as Shabeni, Shirimantanga and Napi, that punctuate the region. Granite is a course-grained rock that is formed when magma cools slowly beneath the surface, and large quartz crystals comprise 27 per cent of the rock. Soils formed on granite are sandy in nature and are deficient in the nutrients required by many plants. By way of comparison, the clay soils around Satara Camp contain 10 times as much calcium and 180 times more phosphates than do granite soils.

The many ochre-coloured granite outcrops, framed by mountain rock figs (*Ficus glumosa*), offer an ideal habitat for klipspringer, baboon and leopard, while rock hyrax occur in one locality west of Berg-en-dal. One of the Park's unsolved mysteries is that in the Southern Region rock hyrax are restricted to the Ntlokweni Hills – despite an abundance of suitable habitat throughout the region. This population has remained in the same locality for the past 35 years, failing to colonise adjacent, ideal habitat. This is difficult to explain as rock hyrax also occur north of the Olifants River.

The Lebombo Motorised 4x4 Eco-Trail follows the eastern boundary of the Park for 515 kilometres, from Crocodile Bridge to Pafuri.

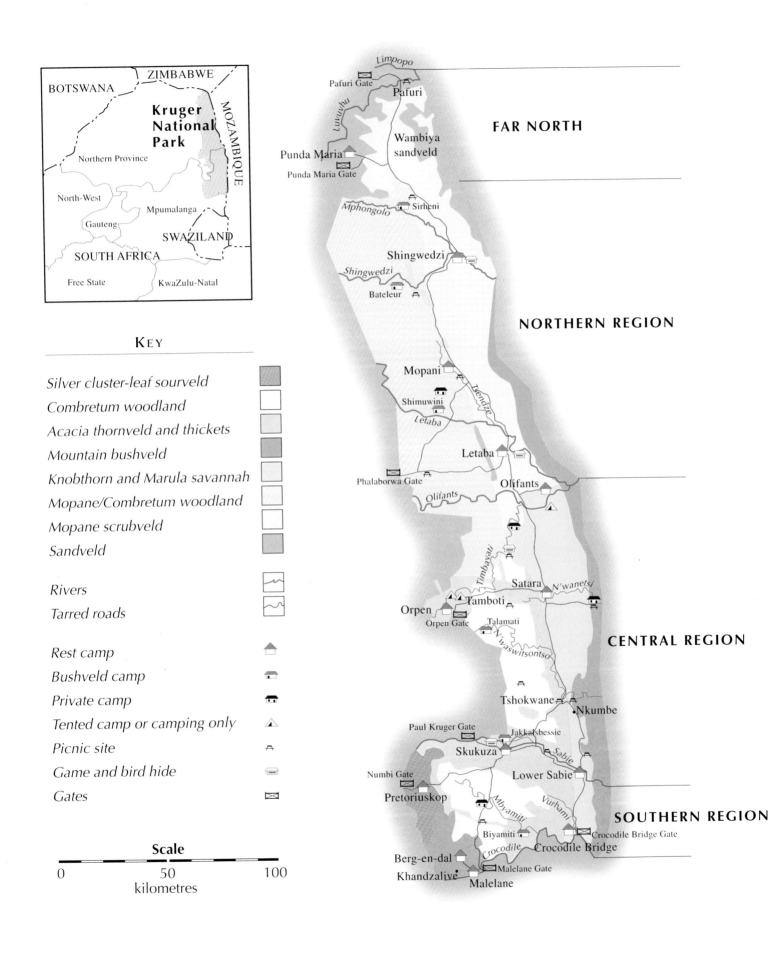

Kruger National Park

BOTSWANA
ZIMBABWE
MOZAMBIQUE
Northern Province
North-West
Mpumalanga
Gauteng
SWAZILAND
SOUTH AFRICA
Free State
KwaZulu-Natal

KEY

Silver cluster-leaf sourveld
Combretum woodland
Acacia thornveld and thickets
Mountain bushveld
Knobthorn and Marula savannah
Mopane/Combretum woodland
Mopane scrubveld
Sandveld

Rivers
Tarred roads

Rest camp
Bushveld camp
Private camp
Tented camp or camping only
Picnic site
Game and bird hide
Gates

Scale

0   50   100
kilometres

Limpopo
Pafuri Gate
Pafuri

FAR NORTH

Wambiya
sandveld

Punda Maria
Punda Maria Gate

Luvuvhu

Mphongolo
Sirheni

Shingwedzi

NORTHERN REGION

Shingwedzi
Bateleur

Mopani
Shimuwini

Letsitele / Letaba

Letaba
Tshendze

Phalaborwa Gate
Olifants

Olifants

Timbavati

Satara
N'wanetsi

Orpen
Tamboti
Orpen Gate
Talamati

N'waswitsontso

CENTRAL REGION

Tshokwane
Nkumbe

Paul Kruger Gate
Jakkalsbessie

Skukuza
Sabie
Lower Sabie

Numbi Gate

Pretoriuskop
Mbyamiti
Vurhami

SOUTHERN REGION

Biyamiti
Crocodile Bridge
Crocodile Bridge Gate

Berg-en-dal
Crocodile
Malelane Gate
Khandzalive
Malelane

Pretoriuskop Area

On higher-lying terrain, in the vicinity of Pretoriuskop, a coarse sandy soil containing many quartz particles is formed on weathered granite. As a result, the dominant vegetation is a silver cluster-leaf (*Terminalia sericea*) sourveld characterised by tall stands of *Hyparrhenia* spp., a 'sour grass' that is only palatable to game when it is young or recently burnt. When, prior to 1923, sheep farmers were granted grazing rights in the area, the veld was burned annually and an open savanna was maintained by fire. As annual rainfall here is high for the Park, averaging 744 millimetres, grass grew profusely and large herds of grazers were drawn to the area.

When Colonel Sandenbergh succeeded James Stevenson-Hamilton in 1946 he immediately banned all controlled veld fires until 1954. In this high-rainfall area much of the vegetation had been held in a subclimax condition by regular fires, and once fires were excluded thatch grass grew into tall stands. Trees were able to grow to a height where fire was no longer a major limiting factor on their growth, and a silver cluster-leaf woodland rapidly replaced the open savanna. Because the leaves of silver cluster-leafs are seldom eaten by browsers, these animals have left the area, as have the large herds of zebra and wildebeest that frequented what was once open grassland. Despite later policy reversals, the open savanna conditions which once prevailed have never been restored. The network of circular roads around the camp is a legacy from the days when Pretoriuskop offered some of the best game-viewing in Kruger.

While it boasts no large herds of grazers, the Pretoriuskop area provides valuable habitat for the magnificent jet-black sable and fawn-coloured reedbuck, both antelope with specific habitat requirements that include tall grassland and an open woodland. Since 1986 there has been a considerable and worrying decrease in sable in Kruger, and this region provides an important habitat for this regal antelope. Reedbuck have also suffered in the past from bush encroachment and a reduction in tall grasslands, and about half of the Kruger population can be found on the vleis that occur along water courses in the Pretoriuskop area.

The majority of the white rhino found in Kruger occur in the Southern Region. The most successful of the eight mammal species re-introduced into Kruger since the 1960s, white rhino were already extinct in the Lowveld by 1896. Between 1961 and 1972 a total of 337 were translocated from Hluhluwe-Umfolozi Park in KwaZulu-Natal, and the majority were released in the Southern Region. White rhino are bulk grazers and are able to utilise grasses that are not highly nutritious. Assisted by an abundant food source, they have responded well to protection and now number more than 2 600, representing the largest population in Africa.

The Pretoriuskop region is also noted for an abundance of trees and some species, such as the large-leaved false-thorn (*Albizia versicolor*) and Mobola plum (*Parinari curatellifolia*), occur only on the deep sandy soils found here and in the Far North. Fine specimens of teak (*Pterocarpus angolensis*), wild olive (*Olea europaea*) and Transvaal beech (*Faurea saligna*) also occur here. Because these trees are rare elsewhere in Kruger, it was at one time policy to protect them by restricting

the elephant population in the Southern Region to 900. One species of combretum, the false forest bushwillow (*Combretum woodii*), is restricted to Ship Mountain. Near the foot of this hull-shaped mountain, an old wagon trail crossing a stream marks the birthplace of Jock of the Bushveld, in 1885.

The woodlands around Pretoriuskop are home to several bird species that have a limited distribution in the Park. These include 'middleveld' species such as the black sunbird, yellowfronted tinker barbet and Ayres' cisticola. Other notable bird records for the area include the pennantwinged nightjar, redcollared widow and gorgeous bush shrike.

Combretum Woodlands

Between the high-lying woodlands of Pretoriuskop and the low-lying acacia thickets in the east, the middle slopes comprise the major portion of the Southern Region and are clothed in a dense woodland of combretum and marula trees. In total, 14 species and subspecies of *Combretaceae* occur in the Kruger National Park, and of these, the red bushwillow (*Combretum apiculatum*) is particularly abundant. After the mopane of the semi-arid Northern Region, this is the most common tree in the Kruger Park, and its leaves are browsed by kudu, giraffe and elephant.

Most of Kruger's white rhino occur in the Southern Region. The best sightings are around Pretoriuskop, Mbyamiti River, and south of Lower Sabie.

Although this woodland does not sustain the concentrations of game found on 'sweet grasses' underpinned by clay soils, reasonable populations of impala, kudu, zebra, giraffe, buffalo, white rhino and elephant are present. As wildebeest and zebra – preferred prey species of lion – are found in low numbers in the Southern Region, lion are less common than they are in the Central Region. This relative scarcity of lion means that cheetah and wild dog occur in reasonable numbers. A recent survey found that about half of Kruger's 180 cheetah occur in the Southern Region, even though the Central Region offers exceptional habitat for them. Likewise, wild dog are most common in the mountainous terrain near Berg-en-dal, although their favourite prey, impala, concentrate on acacia veld near the Sabie and Crocodile rivers.

Another common predator found in bushwillow woodland is the leopard, although these superbly camouflaged cats are not often seen. The numerous rocky outcrops, dense foliage and an ample supply of medium-sized mammals make the area ideal for their hunting technique of stalking and ambushing prey. As leopards are solitary and often store their prey in tree canopies out of the reach of other predators, they are able to survive in a wide variety of habitats.

In recent years several leopard attacks on staff have been reported in Kruger. One of the most publicised attacks took place on the night of 21 August 1998 on the bridge crossing the Matjulu River near Malelane Camp. Student ranger Charles Swart was guiding 12 visitors on a night drive when he stopped the vehicle on the bridge. Holding his rifle in one hand, Swart was standing a short distance behind the vehicle when the leopard attacked and killed him.

Wild dog may be seen on the road between Berg-en-dal and Skukuza.

Seasonal Rivers

Many seasonal rivers flow across this region and their sandy beds often hold pools of water that attract a wide variety of game. The appealing Mbyamiti is the largest of these rivers and its catchment falls entirely within the Park. Other important water courses in the region include the N'watimhiri, N'waswitshaka, Mtshawu, Mlambabe and Vurhami. When summer thunderstorms over high-lying country produce sudden downpours, surface water may flow down sandy riverbeds for several weeks. Tall apple-leaf (*Lonchocarpus capassa*) and jackal-berry (*Diospyros mespiliformis*) trees line the banks of these water courses, their roots probing deep below the surface to reach the water table, so that even in periods of drought these trees are able to retain their foliage.

Giraffe are little affected by severe drought conditions, and survive by concentrating their feeding patterns along river banks. Other mammals and birds are also drawn to the riverbeds, for a variety of reasons. Fruit-bearing trees such as wild figs and jackal-berries are common here and attract fruit-eating birds. An accumulation of clay along river courses yields sweet grasses, and the presence of trees like the brack thorn (*Acacia robusta*) and buffalo thorn (*Ziziphus mucronata*) attracts a variety of browsers.

To the east and north of the bushwillow woodland, along the perennial Sabie and Crocodile rivers, acacia woodland is found on flat land near rivers and sustains an abundance of wildlife. Impala are particularly abundant, and heavily grazed clearings are a common feature of the thorn thickets. When Stevenson-Hamilton journeyed into the Sabi Game Reserve for the first time in 1902 he came across his first impala herd in this vegetation type near Renosterkoppies, and today 30 per cent of the total population still occurs in the Southern Region. The destructive feeding habits of the concentrations of elephant and buffalo found near to rivers actually helps to make the habitat more suitable for impala. Although acacias are heavily browsed by impala, on fertile clay soils the trees easily replace leaves consumed. If conditions are suitable some species of acacia, such as the horned thorn (*Acacia grandicornuta*), which is common along the Sabie River, can flower several times during one season.

The Sabie River is a veritable magnet for wildlife. When it enters the Park near Phabeni, the Sabie surges over granite outcrops and then, from Skukuza onwards, the river flows more gently, its channels carving islands crowded with matumis (*Breonadia salicina*) and its banks shaded by enormous sycamore figs (*Ficus sycomorus*). The Sabie River, and the corridor of riverine bush that grows luxuriantly along its

The Sabie River surges over granite outcrops before following a gentle course bounded by reed-lined sandbanks.

banks, provides essential habitat for a wide diversity of game including hippo, bushbuck, kudu, waterbuck, grey duiker, vervet monkey, baboon, elephant, buffalo, lion and leopard. The 43-kilometre road between Skukuza, the Park's headquarters and its largest camp, and Lower Sabie, one of the most popular and picturesque camps, is the most popular game-viewing road in the whole of Kruger. Although the Southern Region comprises one-fifth of the total area of the Park, 43 per cent of all hutted accommodation and four of the nine biggest rest camps are concentrated here, which is a measure of its popularity.

At the end of winter herds of game congregate near the Sabie once minor water courses have dried up. The river is home to in the region of 600 hippo, a large population of crocodiles and the Lowveld largemouth (*Serranochromis meridianus*), an olive-brown endemic fish weighing up to 1.2 kilograms, that is virtually restricted to the Sabie.

The Sabie River is a superb locality for bird-watching, and many species are attracted by the rich habitat provided by permanent water and riverine forest. Among the riverine bird species found here that are uncommon elsewhere in the Park are the purplecrested lourie, green pigeon, African finfoot, African goshawk, fish eagle, whitecrowned plover, black duck, halfcollared kingfisher, whitefronted bee-eater, trumpeter hornbill, Natal robin and bearded robin.

Hippos play an important role in the ecology of the Sabie River.

Green pigeons roost in the tree canopy sustained by the Sabie River.

In terms of biodiversity the Sabie is the richest river in the country, but the river has not always been in such pristine condition. In 1922 Stevenson-Hamilton remarked on the poor state of the Sabie River. Gold mines in its upper reaches were the culprits, and pollution increased to the extent where the river became sterile. In 1933 a water expert found no evidence of micro-organisms in the river, and boreholes had to be drilled to supply Skukuza with water. The Department of Mining argued that too many jobs were dependent on mining to do anything about this, and it was only after World War II that steps were taken to prevent pollution.

THE CENTRAL REGION:
GAME-FILLED SAVANNAS

The land between the Sabie and Olifants rivers comprises the Central Region, 5 849 square kilometres of open savanna, which encompasses some of the best wildlife habitat in the whole of the Kruger Park. The sweet grasses that grow on fertile soils formed on shale and volcanic basalt, and an abundance of excellent browsing trees, sustain the largest impala, buffalo, giraffe, kudu, wildebeest, zebra, waterbuck and sable populations in the Park. Although this region makes up only 30 per cent of the Park's surface area, it accounts for 40 per cent of its total biomass, supports nearly half of the Park's lion and sizeable numbers of leopard, hyaena and cheetah.

A belt of granite in the west of this region ends roughly in line with the main road from Skukuza to Olifants camps, bordering an extensive intrusion of basalt that extends eastward to the Lebombo Mountains. This latter region produces clay soils that are rich in the elements required by plants. The savanna here is dominated by marula (*Sclerocarya birrea*) and knobthorn (*Acacia nigrescens*) trees scattered across sweet veld, and browsers find these species particularly palatable. Apart from their edible fruit, which is eaten by many animals, elephants eat the leaves and bark of the marula, and the larvae of eight species of butterfly are known to feed on its foliage. Giraffe and kudu are especially partial to knobthorns, but avoid competition for the same food source by feeding at different heights. About 30 per cent of the giraffe's diet is made up of knobthorn leaves, and in some parts of the Central Region giraffe densities are as high as one animal per two square kilometres.

Apart from elephants, which are now widely distributed throughout the region, the black rhino is an important browser that is seldom seen. Between 1980 and 1989 groups of black rhino from KwaZulu-Natal were released at Kumana, Leeupan and along the Sweni River. Although it is difficult to count these retiring animals, it would appear as if a stable population is now present in the Central Region.

The basalt plains support a wealth of birds, but several species exhibit a particular preference for this habitat. These include pallid harrier, secretary bird, ostrich, kori bustard, redbacked mannikin, Swainson's francolin, chestnutbacked finchlark, doublebanded sandgrouse and wattled starling.

Fences and Foot-and-Mouth

The inclusion of the game-rich Central Region was the most difficult part of the negotiations that led to the proclamation of the Kruger National Park in 1926. All the land between the Sabie and Olifants rivers had previously been surveyed into farms, although conditions were not conducive for settled agriculture at the time. Most of the land around Satara belonged to the state and could be incorporated, but to the north and south 33 privately-owned and 49 company-owned farms, mostly the property of the Transvaal Consolidated Land Company, had to be expropriated or exchanged for land elsewhere. The Kruger Park's uneven western boundary was therefore decided more by the need to limit the number of farms the government needed to purchase, than it was by any ecological consideration. Between 1935 and 1944, Eileen Orpen bought seven farms covering 24 529 hectares to extend the western boundary, but even such a generous gift did not include enough land to adequately support the Park's migratory herds.

When a fence was erected in 1960 by the state veterinary authority to prevent the spread of foot-and-mouth disease to cattle from game, game herds were cut off from their favoured summer grazing lands. Between 1969 and 1977 the

Giraffe are partial to knobthorn leaves, and in parts of the Central Region densities are as high as one animal per two square kilometres.

wildebeest populations (three herds) in the central district dropped by 68 per cent. A wet cycle made it worse by causing above-average growth of grass; wildebeest prefer to graze shorter grass, and lion can stalk them with ease through long grass.

Park managers incorrectly blamed lion and wet cycles for this drastic decline in numbers, but the fence turned out to be the main culprit. More thorough investigation revealed that the western herd, which used to migrate from the Sabie area in winter to the Timbavati area northwest of Orpen, had suffered the most, plummeting by 90 per cent.

The wildebeest subsequently responded favourably to a dry cycle, and the fence was removed in 1994, but the case study was evidence of the complexity of the ecosystem and the knock-on effect that a single action can have on population dynamics. Just erecting a fence can play havoc with a system by disrupting migratory patterns, as has been the case all over Africa – and especially in Botswana.

Five seasonal rivers meander across the Central Region and, as wildlife is abundant, during intense dry cycles water supplies are often depleted. The Timbavati River was perennial in the early days, but forestry, agriculture and habitat degradation beyond the Park's boundaries drastically reduced its flow. Despite these factors, large pools still occurred in the river and for a time two were deep enough to support herds of hippos. But runoff from overgrazed lands upstream silted up the pools in the mid-1960s, and the river ceased to be a reliable source of water.

This pattern of pools silting up and rivers becoming more erratic was well documented by Park rangers, and as a result many man-made dams and water holes were established in the Central Region. Some of these water points complicated an already complex situation by concentrating game herds in areas that were traditionally utilised only during summer. Many of the water holes and dams have become popular tourist attractions, but water holes established far from riverbeds, and in areas that would have been waterless in winter, were incorrectly placed. Some of the most important dams in the Central Region were built in the Park's early, formative years. These include Kumana (1935), Mazithi (1936), Orpen (1945), Mlondozi (1951), Gudzani (1952), Ngwenyeni and Vutomi (1956).

Predator Paradise

The concentration of predators, especially lions, in the Central Region ensures that it remains a popular tourist destination. As a result there are many camps in the region. Situated in the centre of the region, Satara is the second largest camp in Kruger, and there are also two smaller rest camps, the charming Tamboti Tented Camp, a camping and caravan camp, two private camps and two bushveld camps.

Satara, the Central Region's largest camp, accommodates 434 visitors.

No fewer than 60 lion prides occupy home ranges in the Central Region, with an average pride size of 12 lions, and within a 20 kilometre radius of Satara 22, lion prides have been counted. An adult lion requires about nine zebra per year, or the equivalent prey weighing 1 500 kilograms, and lion kill on average every three to four days. The size of a lion pride's territory ranges from 20 to about 400 square kilometres, depending on food availability, but in the Central Region territories are generally not much larger than 80 square kilometres. Studies have shown that lion are opportunistic hunters and will alter the prey they select in times of drought. A study of 257 lion in the Central Region found that giraffe, wildebeest and zebra provided 81 per cent of all food consumed, but accounted for only half of kills made due to the large size of these animals. In times of

drought, lion preyed heavily on buffalo and less so on zebra and wildebeest, but zebra normally comprise one-seventh of lion kills. Mostly zebra foals are killed by lions, but in the case of wildebeest, animals of all ages are caught. In response to lion attacks, the 12 000-strong zebra in the region give birth to about 4 000 foals each year and are able to withstand predation, but do not thrive during wet cycles as they require grass of a medium length. Zebra and wildebeest, therefore, are two species that do best when rainfall is below normal.

The high density of lions in the region, estimated at about 13 per 100 square kilometres, has major repercussions for two of Kruger's rare predators. Only 60 cheetah have been observed over the entire region, although their favourite prey is abundant and the open savannas provide ideal opportunities for hunting. A census found that adult cheetah also outnumber young animals, and the ratio of females without cubs to mothers with cubs was higher when compared to other regions, which is indicative of a population that is sparsely distributed. The overall density of cheetah in the Central Region is only half that of the Southern Region, which contains less ideal habitat. Where new parks have been established elsewhere in South Africa, and the full component of predators has been re-introduced, many of the released cheetahs have fallen victim to lion attacks.

The density of lion also negatively affects the distribution of the endangered wild dog. Wild dog are highly endangered and occur in only 13 African countries. With a total population numbering less than 5 000, only six populations including Kruger's contain more than 100 dogs. However, more than 80 per cent of wild dog in the Park are younger than four years of age, and very few live to the age of seven years, which indicates that disease and predation are exacting a heavy toll.

A comprehensive survey located only six packs throughout the Central Region, and almost all of these packs were found on the sandy granite soils that occur in a south to north band stretching from the Sabie River northward along the Hlanguleni road to the Olifants River. On the fertile eastern plains, where wildlife is plentiful, wild dog are seldom seen. Is this because wild dog prefer sandy conditions to clay soil? One explanation suggested that, as wild dog prey primarily on impala in Kruger, they are concentrated in red bush-willow woodland because impala are common in this vegetation type. This is unlikely, however, as impala reach their highest densities in acacia thickets near water. Further investigation found that lion show a marked preference for marula savanna, which is widespread on the eastern plains, and wild dog were most common in mountainous country and sour bushveld. As lion account for at least one third of wild dog pup deaths, wild dog actively avoid areas where lion are common, even when their favourite prey is plentiful in these parts, and will move their puppies to new dens to avoid predation.

Although cheetah and wild dog do not thrive where lion are numerous, spotted hyaena are able to hold their own. One estimate concluded that there were at least 1 200 spotted hyaena in the Central Region, an even larger population than that of their major competitor. In November, when the impala give birth, many hyaena feed exclusively on young impala. Hyaena clans are strongly territorial and show evidence of a robust female-dominated hierarchy. In the Central Region they do not attack large mammals, as is the case in East Africa, and are able to survive adequately by preying on small animals and scavenging the remains of lion kills.

THE NORTHERN REGION: ENDLESS PLAINS OF MOPANE

A low-lying, sun-baked plain ranging in elevation from 300 to 450 metres, the Northern Region extends north of the Olifants River. This semi-arid region, covering 7 000 square kilometres, is relatively close to the warm, moisture-laden air currents of the Indian Ocean, and yet annual rainfall for the most part varies from 400 to 500 millimetres. Average rainfall for Olifants Camp is 478 millimetres, 523 millimetres for Shingwedzi Camp, and only in the months from November to February does more than 50 millimetres fall in any one month. The extreme aridity of this region – which is located near to ample sources of oceanic moisture – is attributed to the Limpopo high pressure system, which causes air to descend and therefore acts as a barrier to air moving in from the coast.

Of all the regions of Kruger, the vegetation in the north is the least diversified and much of the region is blanketed in shrub mopane (*Colophospermum mopane*). The distribution

Lined by fig trees, a quiet channel of the Olifants River carves a verdant swathe across the sun-baked mopane country of the Northern Region.

of this tree in South Africa, Mozambique and Zimbabwe coincides with hot, semi-arid, low-lying valleys, and the mopane thrives under these conditions. Mopane leaves hang vertically and during the heat of the day very little shade is cast, which helps to minimise evaporation. Where soils are deep and adequate water is available this tree can grow into a fine specimen, but where soils are shallow or poorly drained the mopane grows as a multi-stemmed shrub. Not many browsers feed on its leaves, but they form an important part of elephants' diet. Caterpillars of the emperor moth (*Imbrasia belina*), also known as mopane worms, feed on the leaves and are considered a delicacy by many African tribes.

Although water use beyond the Park's boundary has reduced its flow, the Letaba remains one of the most enchanting of the Kruger National Park's seven major rivers.

Across this almost homogeneous expanse of mopane, the Olifants, Letaba, Shingwedzi, Tsendze and Mphongolo rivers carve corridors of botanical diversity. Along their banks, tall apple-leaf, sycamore fig, nyala (*Xanthocercis zambesiaca*), tamboti (*Spirostachys africana*) and jackal-berry trees form narrow corridors that differ markedly from the surrounding stunted mopane. Apart from the Olifants and Letaba, these rivers hold water mainly in the form of large pools. The

Olifants River is the largest in Kruger and its considerable catchment, extending over 54 300 square kilometres, generates four per cent of the total river flow in South Africa.

During the severe drought of the mid-1940s, the Letaba stopped flowing for two short spells at the end of winter. The Letaba and Olifants rivers are home to 60 per cent of the Park's hippo, and in the past large numbers of hippo died in times of drought. In 1970 the American industrialist, Charles Engelhard, financed the construction of a large dam on the Letaba River downstream of Letaba Camp. The completion of major reservoirs has helped create suitable habitat for both hippos and waterbirds. Since the completion of the Engelhard Dam, three other dams have been built on the Letaba and the completion of the Kanniedood Dam on the Shingwedzi River in 1975 pushed back water in the riverbed for six kilometres. While these reservoirs are artificial structures, and not entirely in keeping with the principles of a national park, in an arid region where the supply of water from outside has become erratic (nowadays, surface flow ceases in early May in most years), these dams at least make it possible to retain the many water-dependent species that would otherwise die out.

These relatively lush river corridors are the favourite habitat of many species of mammals and birds. Waterbuck, bushbuck, impala and kudu are common, but the riverine vegetation is also the haunt of the exquisite nyala. Herds of elephant and buffalo depend on the rivers for water, and predators such as lion, leopard and hyaena concentrate where prey is abundant. The Northern Region is home to half of Kruger's elephants. Breeding herds favour the country bordering the Olifants River, and elephant herds also gather along the Letaba, Shingwedzi and Mphongolo rivers. Elephants consume vast quantities of water, and spend the heat of the day cooling off in rivers wherever sufficient water can be found.

Since the proclamation of the first conservation area in the Lowveld in 1898, the elephant population has enjoyed a phenomenal increase. In 1905 Stevenson-Hamilton estimated that there were only 10 elephants in the Park; by 1932 there were 170, and at the time of his retirement in 1946 the population had reached 450. The current estimate of just less than 9 000 represents a remarkable recovery. In addition to the fact that elephants have been able to raise their young in the safety afforded by the Park, immigration from Mozambique, where poaching has been rife, has also played a major contributing role in this increase in the Park's population.

As game in the region is concentrated near water, tourist camps and roads also tend to be located near rivers or major dams. Olifants, Letaba and Shingwedzi camps all border on rivers of the same names, and the Shimuwini, Bateleur and Sirheni bushveld camps are all positioned near large dams. In this sunburnt region where summer temperatures of 45°C are not uncommon, wildlife is drawn to the rivers, and any exploration of these picturesque river roads, especially along the Olifants and Shingwedzi rivers, can produce some of the best game-viewing in the Park. Apart from the concentrations of game that are present, the towering shade trees and refreshing pools of fast-flowing water, adjacent to sunbaked mopaneveld, create some of the most appealing habitats in all of Kruger.

Apart from the sizeable herds of elephant and buffalo that inhabit the mopaneveld, the eastern basalt plains are the chosen habitat for several rare antelope species. Of the 20 species of antelope that occur in the Park, a number of species are restricted to the Northern Region. Broad, grass-covered drainage lines are a common feature of the shrub mopaneveld. These grasslands are formed when clay soil formed on basalt coincides with a deeper layer of

A few rare roan antelope survive on the northern plains.

Large herds of Cape buffalo are a common feature of the northern mopaneveld.

impervious calcareous substrate. Trees cannot take root and elongated, narrow grasslands are formed that provide optimum habitat for tsessebe, sable, roan, eland and reedbuck. But in times of severe drought, grass cannot obtain sufficient moisture to grow, and barren areas of exposed soil result. In areas where dry spells have killed off the grass, major declines in these rare antelope species occur. Following the severe drought of 1992/1993, sable decreased by 85 per cent and tsessebe by 70 per cent in the Northern Region. As these antelope are rare in South Africa, park managers are concerned and have taken steps to arrest the decline. Recovery in populations is normally fairly rapid in the wet cycle that follows a long drought, however, providing that long-term changes in the habitat were not caused by the drought.

Many species of birds have a preference for a specific habitat, and a number of unusual birds can be found in the Northern Region. The mourning dove has a distinct preference for rest camps and is common in Letaba and Shingwedzi camps. Arnot's chat is restricted to tall mopane forest, and in Kruger the greyrumped swallow and brown-throated martin occur only along the Olifants and Letaba rivers. Where the Olifants cuts a gorge through the Lebombo, goliath heron, Cape parrot, yellowbellied bulbul, yellow-spotted nicator and black stork build nests, and shrub mopaneveld can reveal Dickinson's kestrel, marsh owl, rock kestrel, cloud cisticola and broadbilled roller.

THE FAR NORTH:
RARE BIRDS AND SAND FOREST

This region embraces several fascinating ecozones that differ markedly from habitats elsewhere in the Park. A total of 15 distinct plant communities have been identified and these are the product of a combination of many diverse factors. As this is Kruger's northernmost extremity, located 22°30' south of the equator, many tropical elements are present. Part of the region lies in a rain shadow, and Pafuri receives a meagre rainfall of just 362 millimetres a year, so many species from the arid west occur here. A number of rich plant communities coincide with significant areas of sand formed by river flood plains, the Mozambique coastal plain and sandstone formations, and the Luvuvhu River creates a corridor of riverine forest that harbours many forest-dwelling species.

These diverse factors influence the distribution of animals, and many species occur only in the extreme north. The Kruger knocking sand frog (*Tomopterna krugerensis*), named for its wooden, 'knocking' note repeated four to five times a second, is restricted to pans in the area. Bats are

especially well represented, and 13 species occur only in this part of Kruger, including the Egyptian fruit bat, Wood's slit-faced bat and the Madagascar large free-tailed bat. The largely nocturnal bushpig and the rare Sharpe's grysbok attain their highest densities in the Park in this region, and in the 1980s a total of 95 samango monkeys were released in riverine forest at Pafuri, where they have since formed small troops. Apart from the more common animals such as impala, bushbuck, kudu, nyala and buffalo, five packs of endangered wild dog have been observed in the area.

Bushpig are plentiful in undergrowth bordering the Luvuvhu River.

The sandveld communities are among some of the most interesting habitats of the region. West of Punda Maria, sandstone hills and densely wooded flat areas are the dominant natural features. The plant communities found here are very diverse, and no single tree predominates. In Punda Maria Camp itself no less than 80 tree species have been identified. These sandstone hills are the only locality in Kruger for the Natal red hare and yellow-spotted rock dassie (or hyrax).

The sandveld communities around Punda Maria are derived from sandstone, but near the eastern border the Wambiya sandveld is formed on coastal plain sand from Mozambique. Termite mounds are a prominent feature and they support dense thickets that are the only known habitat in Kruger of the tiny suni antelope. Attempts have been made over the years to introduce additional suni from KwaZulu-Natal, but they remain extremely rare.

A total of 23 major pans are scattered across the Wambiya sandveld (see map), which are home to tropical warm-water fish found at the extreme inland limits of their distribution.

The rainbow killifish (*Nothobranchius rachovii*), is a bright red, popular aquarium fish, up to six centimetres in length, that is found nowhere else in South Africa. Spotted killifish (*Nothobranchius orthonotus*), and the peculiar lungfish (*Protopterus annectens*) which has a lung for breathing air and can survive in a mud cocoon at the bottom of a dry pan, are restricted to temporary pans in the vicinity. Apart from these unusual fish, the Cape hare, fawn-coloured lark and pink-throated twinspot only occur in this sandveld, in the Park.

The Luvuvhu flows through a rugged sandstone gorge after it enters the Park, and then lazily meanders across the flood plain at Pafuri, 47 kilometres north of Punda Maria, before meeting the mighty Limpopo. At Pafuri a band of riverine forest grows on alluvial sands along the river bank. Pafuri is regarded by some visitors as the most enchanting corner of the Kruger Park. Part of the area's charm lies in its remoteness, 613 kilometres from Johannesburg and 360 kilometres north of Skukuza, but the occurrence of the sycamore fig, fever tree, nyala, samango monkey and crested guineafowl link the area to the intriguing pockets of sand forest of Maputaland in northern KwaZulu-Natal.

The picnic site on the banks of the Luvuvhu River is a favourite destination for bird enthusiasts, and the brilliant crimson-and-green narina trogon is often seen along the path that follows the river bank. Other notable bird sightings in the area include longtailed starling, wood dove and white-fronted bee-eater. Pafuri is the most important locality for birds in Kruger, especially for rare vagrants and birds from tropical Africa. In total, 29 species or six per cent of the birds recorded in the Park have only been sighted at Pafuri. Some of these avian rarities include trumpeter hornbill, Cape parrot, tropical boubou, Mashona hyliota, broadbilled roller, olive bush shrike, threebanded courser, cinnamon dove, mottled spinetail and yellow white-eye.

A termite mound in the mopaneveld will later provide a home to either warthog, spotted hyaena, wild dog or dwarf mongoose.

LAND CLAIMS AND PEACE PARKS

In December 1998, a Land Claims Court returned the triangle of land between the Luvuvhu and Limpopo rivers, in the far northern corner of the Park, to the Makuleke people. The Makuleke had been removed from the area in 1969 and settled elsewhere, and the land was incorporated into Kruger. In terms of a new agreement the area will now be jointly managed by the Kruger Park and the Makuleke for 25 years, and the community has been granted full rights to all tourism development, but will not settle on the land. This agreement made it possible to incorporate an additional 5 000 hectares of land into Kruger, and helped focus attention on the need to involve local rural communities in wildlife conservation.

A major initiative, led by the Peace Parks Foundation, is the proposed immense Kruger/Banhine-Zinave/ Gonarezhou Transfrontier Conservation Area (TFCA), encompassing a vast

A tranquil pool in the Luvuvhu River provides a sharp contrast to the dead sycamore figs, killed by severe droughts, that line its banks.

95 712 square kilometres, which is larger than Austria or the USA's State of Indiana. The most ambitious of the Foundation's proposed transfrontier parks, it combines four existing national parks, controlled hunting areas and communal lands in South Africa, Mozambique and Zimbabwe. Much of the land is in Mozambique, where rural districts would benefit immensely from ecotourism and job creation.

The Kruger Park receives nearly one million visitors a year, and cannot expand tourist facilities without negatively impacting on the environment. A major new airport has been completed west of Kruger (near Hoedspruit), but all of

the Park's daily spare accommodation would be absorbed by the arrival of a single large passenger jet. Additional camps are needed to accommodate foreign tourists, and the proposed conservation area could sustain over one million wild animals, and would be able to accommodate three million tourists annually without any danger of overcrowding. Experts agree that conservation is the best form of land use for the area, and the transfrontier park would make a significant contribution to the local economies of this semi-arid and undeveloped regions. As people are settled in some regions, the proposed transfrontier park would consist of a mosaic of protected areas and resource utilisation zones.

In many parts of Africa poverty poses a major threat to national parks and natural resources, and land-hungry people have often violated park boundaries. The Peace Parks Foundation is confident that a three-pronged approach that addresses the problems of unemployment and poverty, establishes a culture of peace through co-operation between the member countries, and furthers the cause of conservation, will alter this pattern.

On 24 October 1999, the responsible ministers from South Africa, Mozambique and Zimbabwe signed a Memorandum of Understanding, supporting the establishment of a joint management structure that will create one of the largest conservation areas in the world. The agreement established a Ministerial Committee and an International TFCA Technical Committee to oversee the implementation of the agreement. The Technical Committee, comprising officials from the three countries, will prepare a conceptual plan, draft agreement and final management plan by the end of 2001.

The realisation of the dream of this transfrontier park will face certain obstacles, but none greater than those that faced Stevenson-Hamilton in the 1920s. In 1952 Stevenson-Hamilton published a history of his life in the Park, titled *South African Eden – The Kruger National Park*. Despite the vagaries of Nature, onslaughts from crippling droughts, opposition from many quarters and short-sighted decisions by government departments, the Kruger Park has endured and prospered. In part, its success has been built on a tasteful blend of rural architecture, unpretentious facilities, simple outdoor living and sensitive planning set against the backdrop of the unpredictable, untamed and enthralling pageant of Nature. The Park has indeed become a South African Eden. And if it can play a critical role in the creation of an immense conservation area spanning three nations, this 'Eden' will be one worthy of World Heritage status and a wildlife sanctuary unsurpassed anywhere else in the world.

Previous page

A young buffalo depends on the structure of the herd for protection. Buffalo are almost exclusively grazers, and half the Kruger population occurs on the open savannas of the Central Region. These bovids consume large quantities of grass of a moderate quality, and in doing so play a valuable role in the ecosystem by reducing tall grasslands and opening up areas for the antelope that feed only on short grasses. As an adult can weigh more than 750 kilograms, buffalo comprise a quarter of Kruger's total biomass, or live weight of animals. Although lion working together can overpower an adult bull, the availability of sufficient grass is the most important limiting factor on herd size.

Above and Opposite

Under favourable conditions, when game concentrates around water holes and there is a steady supply of prey, a lioness can give birth to a litter of one to five cubs (above) every two years. Within a pride most cubs are born at the same time, mostly between February and April when young prey animals are abundant. This magnificent lion (opposite) was seen hunting early in the morning very close to Skukuza Camp. Since the establishment of the Park in 1898, lion have increased proportionately to a significant increase in their prey species. In the 1920s Stevenson-Hamilton counted 600 lion in the Park. Today, Kruger supports about 2 000, representing one of the largest populations in Africa.

Opposite left

Baboons feed and rest in trees, but they are primarily ground-dwellers and the troop spends much of the day searching for food within a few kilometres of a favourite sleeping site, which is usually a steep cliff or a large tree.

Opposite right

Although they occur throughout Kruger, vervet monkeys show a distinct preference for riverine bush. Vervets are gregarious animals and are normally found in troops numbering up to 20 individuals. They feed in the tree canopy and on the ground, eating a wide variety of plant material including flowers, fruit, berries, roots and leaves.

Right

Towering five metres above the ground and weighing as much as 1 400 kilograms, the giraffe is the tallest animal of the African savanna – yet still falls prey to lion. In the Central Region, where an abundance of acacias concentrates 60 per cent of the giraffe population, a study found they comprise 15 per cent of all lion kills, but account for nearly half of the food eaten by lion.

Above

The blue water lily has a submerged rhizome that roots in the muddy floor of quiet streams and ponds, where the plant provides a protective environment for water insects, frogs and young fish.

Right

Shaded by a fever tree (*Acacia xanthophloea*) a pool in the Mphongolo River in northern Kruger is a valuable source of water in a region where permanent water is scarce. In the surrounding semi-arid mopaneveld, rainfall is erratic and seldom exceeds 450 millimetres a year. In the nineteenth century, the tree's conspicuous yellow bark served as a beacon indicating the presence of water to thirsty travellers. However, as malaria-carrying mosquitoes favoured the same habitat, the fevers that the disease brought on were incorrectly blamed on the tree.

Opposite

In the Kruger Park bushbuck are associated with dense riverine bush, and the road between Skukuza and Lower Sabie offers the best sightings. They are solitary antelope and occupy home ranges that often overlap. Unlike most antelope species, bushbuck are exceptionally tolerant of each other and territorial displays are a rare phenomenon.

Above

The smallest of the antelope most commonly seen in Kruger, steenbok show a marked preference for the open plains in the eastern region of the Park, formed on volcanic basalt. There is some sexual dimorphism, with only male steenbok having horns, and the females being slightly larger than the males.

Left and Above

A martial eagle (left) perches in a tree with a recently caught leguaan (monitor lizard). These large eagles catch a wide variety of prey including guineafowl, ducks, small antelope, hares and reptiles. Although the bateleur eagle (above) hunts a wide range of birds, small mammals and reptiles, it will also scavenge and has been observed stealing food from other eagles and vultures. This eagle spends much of the day on the wing, often swooping in acrobatic flight or circling overhead, behaviour in keeping with its common name, which is French for acrobat.

Opposite

A knobthorn flowers above a small stream – near Olifants Camp – that holds water for a few months into winter. This miniature aquatic ecosystem is a haven for waterbirds, foam-nest frogs and dragonflies, while birds such as black crake and painted snipe favour the dense vegetation along the stream bank.

Below, Opposite below and Right

A blue wildebeest bull maintains his dominance by means of ritual displays intended to intimidate any intruder. When another bull approaches, the territorial bull's rocking-horse gait and swishing tail (below) are meant to dissuade his competitor. If this display fails, the bull drops to his knees and engages in horn-clashing sparring (opposite below). No injuries result from these contests as the impact is absorbed by the bull's solid horn bosses. One of the bulls eventually surrenders and is chased off the territory by the victor (right).

Overleaf

Wildebeest bulls clash at Bangu, an important water hole on the eastern plains. Males are territorial and even where herds migrate over long distances, temporary territories are established.

Opposite

A female cheetah rests after successfully catching and feeding on an impala, this cat's principal prey in Kruger. Cheetah hunt mostly in the early morning or late afternoon, but will also hunt at night when the moon is full. After bringing down an impala, cheetah feed quickly while keeping constant watch for rival predators, and even the arrival of vultures will dislodge them from a kill.

Above

Cheetah are usually solitary, but family parties of a mother and two subadult cubs are common. The cubs are always from the same litter, and leave the mother when about 18 months old and before the next litter is born. Cheetah occupy large home ranges and, despite an abundance of their favourite prey, in no region of the Park does their density exceed one cheetah to every 45 square kilometres.

Members of a wild dog pack spare no time in devouring
an impala that they have just caught. Aware of hyaena
howling nearby, these dogs consumed their kill in under
three minutes, and by the time the hyaena arrived
on the scene there was no sign of the kill. Competition
from other predators, and direct attacks by lion on
both adults and cubs, reduces wild dog numbers even
within optimum habitat.

A complex social arrangement governs wiid dog and they
are able to live in large packs with few signs of conflict.
Wild dog travel over vast distances, but are sedentary for
a three month period when the pups are raised in an
underground den. Some adult members of the pack leave
the den site daily in search of prey. Here, the 'baby-sitters'
encourage a returning hunter to regurgitate food, which is
done for both the pups and their minders.

Left
The shy greenbacked heron belongs to the Ardeidae family, which includes herons, egrets and bitterns. Sixteen members of the family have been recorded in Kruger. As these birds feed mostly on aquatic animals, some species are present only during wet years.

Below
A yellowbilled stork quietly stalks through shallow water in search of fish, frogs, crustaceans and insects, occasionally stirring the bottom of the dam with its feet to disturb prey. These large, attractive birds are associated with rivers, pans and dams.

Opposite
Sunset Dam, just west of Lower Sabie, offers some of the best opportunities for observing waterbirds in the Kruger Park. Buffalo weaver nests adorn the dead tree which also provides a popular roost for yellowbilled storks.

A redbilled oxpecker removes ticks from a female impala, the smallest of the antelope attended by these birds. Small flocks of oxpeckers clamber about the host cleaning ectoparasites from its hide. When startled, they move to the opposite side of the host, and peer over its back at the source of disturbance. Their noisy, hissing alarm calls help to warn the animals they are perched upon of impending danger.

A baboon combs its fur in search of ticks and fleas. In baboon troops this activity is usually performed by other individuals. Apart from keeping the fur free of ticks and fleas, the daily pattern of grooming is vital for the effective functioning of a troop as it maintains the bonds formed between members. Female baboons form alliances, but will also depend on male allies, which they recruit through grooming.

Previous page
With its dextrous trunk, which is composed of 50 000 muscles, an elephant is able to carefully select leaves from among the thorny branches of a thicket of Delagoa thorns (*Acacia delagoensis*).

Left
The bed of the Mphongolo River in northern Kruger is framed by a tall apple-leaf, while flowering knobthorns add a colourful backdrop. Many African people regard the apple-leaf as a rain tree; when sap-sucking aphids pierce its bark, they eject almost pure water that drips down to form a wet patch on the ground.

Above
A grey lourie feeds on the flowers of a knobthorn. Nineteenth-century hunters named these vocal birds 'go-away birds', a reference to their call and their habit of alerting game to the presence of a hunter.

Right

A tree felled by an elephant provides a perfect vantage point for two cheetah males searching for suitable prey. Although they are ill-equipped for climbing, cheetah will climb trees with sloping trunks to survey the surroundings. Male cheetah, usually brothers, form co-operative associations that may last for years.

Below

The black-backed jackal is a scavenger that is often seen on the fringes of a lion or cheetah kill, where it will wait for the opportunity to steal a morsel. An unusual behaviour pattern that has been observed is their tendency to follow larger predators, especially leopard, while emitting a repetitive yapping call that alerts other jackal to the possibility of a kill.

Below
A serval listens attentively for rodents scurrying through the dense grassland of a vlei near Orpen Dam. Serval prey mainly on rodents, especially vlei rats, and show a marked preference for tall grassland habitat situated near water.

Overleaf left
The mane of a dominant pride lion protects the head and neck from injury and deters rival males by making the lion appear more formidable. In East Africa the Maasai people have copied this mask, and warriors wear feathered headdresses to appear taller and more menacing.

Overleaf right
By 1896 white rhino were extinct in the Lowveld, while elsewhere a relic 50 animals survived between the White and Black Umfolozi rivers in Zululand. Successful conservation measures made it possible to re-introduce 337 rhino from 1961 onwards, and the Kruger Park now safeguards the world's largest population.

Previous pages

During the rut, which takes place between April and June, adult impala males establish territories, which they defend by chasing away rival males. Guttural roars followed by protracted snorts can be heard throughout the day and night, as the dominant male defends his territory against intrusions by neighbouring males. If territorial displays are not effective in fending off rivals, the males resort to horn-clashing duels to determine dominance.

Opposite

As night approaches, a warthog descends into a burrow. Warthogs are active during daylight hours, and underground burrows provide protection at night from both cold and predators. Although a pack of wild dog were raising pups in a den adjacent to this one, these predators made no attempt to catch the warthogs and instead tried – unsuccessfully – to chase them away from the site.

Above

Young vervet monkeys are born mainly from October to January after a gestation period of 140 days. Vervets emit distinct alarm barks for different predators, and young monkeys are taught to recognise these warning signals and run for cover. As they share the riverine forest with a host of birds, including one of their major predators – the crowned eagle – young monkeys must quickly learn to distinguish between dangerous and harmless birds.

Previous page

A male waterbuck, followed by an attentive cattle egret, grazes near the Sabie River. Of the 77 species of African antelope, only the waterbuck has a distinctive white ring around the rump. Grasses of a high nutritional quality and a regular supply of water are both essential habitat requirements for these animals. Cattle egrets, the only members of their family that are not closely dependent on water, feed on grasshoppers and other insects disturbed by large antelope.

Opposite

A hippo in the Sabie River displays the fearsome incisors that can inflict serious wounds during territorial contests. Hippo favour deep pools of slow-moving water, and along the Sabie River there are several well-known pools that they have occupied for many years.

Above

The spotted hyaena's powerful jaws can crush bones and slice through thick hides, useful for a scavenger that often feeds on a carcass that has had the tender meat removed by lion. The hyaena's skull is shaped to accommodate the strong muscles that operate the lower jaw.

Below, Right and Opposite bottom

Egyptian geese feed on grass, seeds, aquatic rhizomes and tubers (below). These birds are territorial and will frequently fly up and down a dam to mark their territory (right). Egyptian geese breed throughout the year, and lay their eggs in a nest hidden in dense vegetation. Both sexes take care of the young (opposite bottom), and newly hatched chicks leave the nest six hours after hatching in response to a call from the female.

A lone buffalo bull near Crocodile Bridge. Unlike most antelope species, male buffalo voluntarily leave the breeding herd and rejoin at a later stage. A herd does not occupy a fixed territory, and its favoured home range includes certain areas that are utilised during winter, and an expanded range that is used during summer. Typically, old bulls eventually become permanently separated from the herd to live a solitary existence, or form small bachelor groups, which make up about 5 per cent of the total buffalo population.

The Kruger Park is a stronghold for the endangered wild dog, although nowhere can it be considered common. Researchers have identified 27 packs with an estimated total population of 360 for the entire park. Wild dog have a highly developed social system and produce large numbers of pups, but remain rare even in areas where their favoured prey animals are abundant. While diseases and lion predation are major limiting factors, research has shown that there is a lack of genetic variability in the Kruger population and this may have resulted in inbreeding.

Right

Alert to potential danger, a Burchell's zebra crosses a water course. During the drier winter months zebra usually congregate within seven kilometres of permanent water. As lion are often concealed in dense bush near water holes, zebra approach cautiously to drink.

Overleaf left

Lion keep a close watch on descending vultures in the hope of locating a potential meal. Lion are opportunistic predators that will also scavenge food from other predators, and in this instance were able to locate the vultures and the remains of a kill in less than 20 minutes.

Overleaf right

A herd of impala approaches water. For impala, gathering together in a herd has many advantages: many pairs of eyes and ears are constantly alert to danger, and the chances of being caught by a predator are greatly reduced. In the Kruger Park there are approximately 10 000 impala herds with an average herd size of 11 animals.

The tree squirrel, particularly common in dry woodland, builds a nest in a hole in a tree. The nest is lined with dry leaves, and a squirrel family shares the same nest and rests together in it during the hottest times of the day.

A large stick insect, measuring 16 centimetres in length, raises a protective umbrella-like wing to frighten off any potential predator. Stick insects are masters of camouflage, blending in colour and shape with their favoured habitat of trees and plants. They will even pretend to sway in the wind, the better to convincingly imitate the branch of a tree.

Right

The dwarf mongoose weighs just 300 grams and spends around five hours a day on average searching for insects, spiders and rodents. The remainder of the day is devoted to sleeping at a den in an old termite mound, or grooming other members of the band.

Below

A horned baboon spider photographed in sandveld habitat in Kruger's far north. The baboon spider derives its name from a dense covering of hair that supposedly resembles the coat of a baboon. They are not web-builders, instead relying on speed and agility to catch prey. They dig tunnels in the ground where they rest and care for their young.

Previous page left
A young spotted hyaena rests at a roadside den. Hyaena are largely nocturnal, and form clans dominated by females. Dominant females always feed first at a carcass and return to the den to suckle their pups, which rely on their mother's milk for the first nine months. A hierarchy also exists amongst males, but the highest ranked male is considered inferior to the lowest ranked female.

Previous page right
Safe within the protection afforded by a troop, a baboon finds time to doze for a few minutes. Within the troop vulnerable members are protected from predators by the dominant males. The close associations formed between members are important for ensuring co-operation in locating sufficient food.

Left top
A resident of dams, pans and marshes, the blackwinged stilt feeds by sweeping its bill over the water in search of insects, worms, crustaceans and molluscs. The young are usually raised during the dry winter months in a nest built on the ground, or on top of a mound of vegetation placed in shallow water.

Left
A reed cormorant dries its wings between fishing expeditions. These birds feed on very small frogs and fish weighing no more than a few grams. They usually fish alone, although they roost together in reedbeds and in dead trees.

Opposite
At times unkindly likened to an undertaker, the marabou stork is primarily a scavenger, but its diverse diet includes frogs, snakes, lizards, young crocodiles, fish, rodents, birds and carrion.

Opposite

An elephant drinks from a pool in the Mphongolo River that still holds water during winter months. An elephant can draw 17 litres of water at a time. During winter, elephant are usually concentrated within six kilometres of water and drink on average every two days, consuming between 180 and 400 litres per visit.

Above

Two young elephants play on the soft, cool sandy bed of the Mphongolo River. Elephants live in well-ordered family groups that are usually led by the oldest female, the matriarch. In addition to the matriarch, the group consists of her older female calves, related females and their offspring. Males leave the herd from the age of 12 years.

Above

While leopard inhabit all 16 of Kruger's major vegetation types, the highest densities occur in dense riverine bush bordering rivers such as the Sabie and Shingwedzi.

Right

Although lion spend much of the day resting, a charging lion dispels any doubts about their strength, speed and agility. Most chases are short and do not exceed 200 metres, but a lion can attain a speed of 60 kilometres an hour in a final burst of speed before bringing down prey.

Opposite and Above

A wild dog pup (opposite) displays some of the distinct markings that make it possible to identify individuals. Only one female usually breeds in a pack, but litters of up to 21 pups have been recorded. The pups are raised in an old aardvark or warthog burrow in a termite mound, and are carefully cared for by adults in the pack. Wild dog pups are born after a gestation period of about 70 days, and are suckled by the dominant female (above) for three months, either in the den or near its entrance. Other adult members of the pack take an active part in cleaning the pups, and will return strays to the den. The pups begin to beg for meat from the age of 14 days, and when old enough are led by the adult dogs in search of prey.

Opposite, top and bottom, and Above
The hamerkop is the only member of its family, and this fascinating bird is regarded as an ill omen by many African people (perhaps in part because of its curious mating dance and uncanny appearance). A solitary bird (opposite top), the hamerkop feeds mainly on frogs and fish. It builds a sizeable nest (opposite bottom) from twigs, reeds and weeds, that can weigh as much as 50 kilograms, in the fork of a robust tree (above) or on a cliff. Construction of the nest can take up to six months, and the bird builds an interior chamber and plasters it with mud. A mud-lined entrance tunnel, about 50 centimetres in length, leads to the inner chamber of the nest where between three and five eggs are laid. Both parents feed the nestlings.

Opposite

Baboons give birth to a single infant and are attentive parents. The infant is dependent on the mother for milk for six to eight months. Within the troop, all females are related, and bonds between them are strong. When the mother retreats into dense vegetation to give birth, the other females often gather to watch the event. Other members of the troop enjoy spending time carrying, grooming and playing with the babies.

Above

A cheetah and her two young cubs near Duke water hole south of Lower Sabie. Mother cheetah give birth in tall grass or dense cover. The cubs are carefully hidden for the first few weeks, and the mother moves them frequently to new hiding places to avoid detection by other predators. While the cubs are small, the mother is vulnerable as she has to remain and hunt within a confined area, and is thus less able to avoid attacks from lion.

Above

Hippo are sensitive to sunburn and spend much of
the day resting in water. After dark they travel up to
20 kilometres from water, eating up to 130 kilograms of
grass in one night. When they submerge, special muscles
prevent water from entering their nostrils and ear passages.

Opposite top

A large Nile crocodile emerges from the water to feed on
a hippo calf that had died in Sunset Dam. Crocodiles
prefer fresh food, however, and catfish form the major
portion of their diet. They perform an important ecological
function in keeping the numbers of these hardy fish in
check. During periods of above-average rainfall, crocodiles
colonise dams up to 45 kilometres from perennial rivers.

Opposite bottom

Water leguaan (monitors) forage in rivers for crabs,
mussels, frogs, fish, fledgling birds and crocodile eggs.
The female digs a nest in an active termite mound, where,
aided by the constant temperature and humidity, the eggs
develop. The following summer, the young lizards dig their
way out and head for the nearest water, where they feed
on insects and small frogs.

Previous page

Sunset over the Sabie River, one of the most important rivers in the Kruger Park. The Sabie, at one time the northern boundary of the original Sabi Game Reserve, flows across the Park for 104 kilometres before entering Mozambique through a rocky gorge in the Lebombo range.

Above and Left

A blackshouldered kite hovers over grasslands in search of prey. Rodents comprise 90 per cent of this small raptor's diet and, once a mouse has been spotted, the bird drops with lightning speed with legs extended (left) to seize its prey. A widespread bird of prey, the blackshouldered kite is found in Africa, Madagascar, southern Europe and tropical Asia as far east as New Guinea.

Opposite

The hisses and squeals of the whitebacked vulture (left) are a common sound at the remains of a kill after the larger predators have eaten their fill. These vultures feed mostly on the softer parts of an animal and will follow other scavengers to locate food. The much larger lappetfaced vulture (right) weighs between six and eight kilograms. Its powerful bill is able to tear through tough hide, and lappetfaced dominate all other vultures gathered around a carcass.

Above

Zebra are dependent on water and visit water holes about every 35 hours during winter. Where artificial water holes have been established, zebra herds have increased to the detriment of the rare sable and roan antelope. As zebra prefer grass of a medium height, they were hardly affected by the severe drought of 1992/1993. Because the zebra's digestive system processes grass faster than the chambered stomach of a ruminant – an animal that chews the cud – they can feed on grasses that are poor in nutrition, while rows of incisor teeth allow them to crop short grasses.

Opposite

Impala gather at a water hole in acacia country near Lower Sabie. They have a marked preference for areas where there is a regular supply of water, short grass and dense thickets of shrubs and trees. These conditions are normally encountered near rivers where a concentration of larger animals, such as elephant and buffalo, further improves the habitat for impala. Impala are prolific breeders and are the most abundant mammal in Kruger, but these medium-sized antelope drink less than one quarter of the water consumed by the Park's elephants.

As leopard are primarily nocturnal and active when lion and hyaena are about, these powerful cats have to face strong competition. In the Kruger Park they prey mainly on impala and aggressively defend their kills against rival predators. Essentially ground dwelling, leopard readily climb trees to escape from danger and to store their kills safely out of the reach of other predators. Long believed to be very scarce, in the 1970s an American researcher captured a surprising number of leopard within a few kilometres of Skukuza, and the estimate of the total number in the Park was revised to about 1 000. The number is believed to have remained relatively unchanged up to the present. This is because – barring major habitat changes and human interference – leopard populations tend to remain stable, kept in balance by the availability of prey species and the corresponding size of each leopard's territory.

Opposite and Above

White rhino require a reliable supply of water, both for drinking (every two to three days) and for the protective layer of mud that helps shield their hides from biting insects. In Kruger 85 per cent of the population occurs in the Southern Region, where rainfall is higher than average and water holes are evenly distributed. Their senses of smell and hearing are good, but their eyesight is poor and redbilled oxpeckers (opposite) warn them of potential danger. A white rhino bull marks his territory by spray-urinating (above) along its boundaries. Only territorial males do this; subordinate males are allowed to live within the territory so long as they remain submissive. Females are free to wander across the territories of several males.

Above and Opposite

In an unusual display, a female saddlebilled stork at Sunset Dam near Lower Sabie repeatedly throws a stick into the air and retrieves it amidst much flapping of her wings. These storks breed mainly in February and March, and both sexes build a nest of sticks in the crest of a tree near to water. As there were no other storks present at the dam, it is unlikely that this was courtship behaviour. Perhaps the stork was practising catching fish. These storks feed mainly on fish weighing up to 500 grams, and will also eat frogs, molluscs and reptiles. When feeding, they walk slowly in shallow water stabbing at prey with their long bills, or stand quietly waiting for fish to swim past. After catching a fish, the stork may toss it into the air before catching and swallowing it.

Overleaf left

Giraffe show a distinct preference for knobthorns. Their consistent browsing often prunes the trees into shapes more in keeping with a manicured garden.

Overleaf right

An estimated 29 000 zebra are found in the Kruger Park, with the highest concentrations occurring on the grassy plains of the Central Region.

Above and Opposite, top and bottom
Many animals, especially predators and even antelope such as bushbuck and grey duiker, are active mainly at night and depend on their keen senses of smell and hearing to locate food. The bushpig (above) is a secretive animal associated with reedbeds and dense forest. They are seldom seen, and were thought to occur only along the Luvuvhu River and in restricted localities along the Olifants River. In Percy FitzPatrick's book *Jock of the Bushveld*, set in 1885, bushpig are recorded in the present-day Southern Region, and this individual was recently photographed on the Mbyamiti River near Biyamiti Bushveld Camp.

The civet (opposite top) feeds on a wide variety of small mammals, snakes and even on marula fruit, and helps to distribute the seeds of this, and several other trees. Although fairly common, civet are seldom seen except just before dark. Once detected, they can usually be seen on subsequent days in the same locality.

The large-spotted genet (opposite bottom), a solitary predator that feeds mostly on rodents, is the most common of 10 species of small nocturnal predators that occur in the Park. This genet thrives in well-wooded country near to water.

Opposite, left and right

The regal sable (left), arguably the most beautiful antelope in the Park, has specific habitat requirements that include tall grassland and open woodland. An increase in zebra herds and prolonged drought has caused a considerable decline in sable in recent years. Blue wildebeest (right) favour short grasses and need to drink less than other grazers such as zebra and buffalo. Although wildebeest are dependent on water, the severe drought of 1992/93 had little effect on their population, currently estimated at about 13 000.

Above

A kudu bull displays the longest horns of all the antelope that occur in Kruger. At the age of nine months a male kudu sports two short horns, which begin to grow and curve with age to form the corkscrew shape typical of mature bulls. The record length of 181 centimetres is more than twice that recorded for a close relative, the nyala. There have been several observations of jousting kudu bulls interlocking their spiral horns and being unable to disengage. Unable to disentangle their horns or flee, the helpless contestants soon fall prey to predators.

Rooibosrant Dam, near Bateleur Bushveld Camp, is one of the prettiest in the Park, and an ideal place for watching waterbirds such as whitefaced whistling ducks. Drowned leadwoods (*Combretum imberbe*), in the far distance, can remain in the water for many years as their wood is especially fine grained and very heavy, weighing 1 200 kilograms per cubic metre.

About 2 300 hippo inhabit Kruger's rivers, with the majority of the population sheltering in the Sabie, Olifants and Letaba. Water extraction outside the Park's borders has reduced the flow of the Letaba and Luvuvhu, and these rivers are no longer perennial. In order to guarantee a reliable water supply for wildlife, 65 large dams have been built, creating perfect habitats for hippo.

Above

The yellowbilled hornbill is a common bird that often gathers at picnic sites. During its breeding season in summer, the female is sealed inside a nest in a hollow tree with only a narrow slit for an opening. Food is passed into the nest by the male, who spends much of the day catching insects to feed the female. About 20 days after the first egg has hatched, the female breaks out and the chicks reseal the nest without any help from the parents.

Opposite

The ground hornbill is an intriguing and rare bird that weighs up to four kilograms. It is reluctant to fly, and groups range in size from two to eight birds. It may be seen foraging on the ground for reptiles, frogs, snails and small mammals. Only one female in a group breeds, and she lays two eggs at the beginning of summer in a hollow tree. While attending the eggs, the female is fed by the adult male and sometimes by immature birds.

Previous page

Hyaena have learned to use the culverts under the main roads in Kruger as dens to raise their young. During the heat of the day, especially in summer, these concrete tunnels can become exceptionally hot and the cubs may emerge to rest near the entrance.

Opposite and Above

Play activities within the safety of the pride prepare lion cubs for hunting success in adulthood. Young cubs display a pattern of brown spots and rosettes that is similar to the patterning on the coat of leopard, and may be useful as camouflage.

Top left

Noisy, colourful and conspicuous, the glossy starling feeds on insects, fruit and aloe nectar, as indicated in the photograph. Aloes flower in winter and provide these birds with an ample food source. Starlings often gather at picnic sites, where their resonant calls are an integral part of the Kruger Park's distinct ambience.

Above

The crested barbet bores holes in dead trees and raises its young from August to February. These birds are often seen hopping about on the ground, with tail and crest feathers erect, in search of insects.

Left

The blue waxbill is the most common of the four waxbill species found in the Park. Small groups are often seen foraging for seeds on the ground. They have been known to build their nests near wasps for protection.

Above

The Burchell's coucal's watery call is often heard before the onset of rain, which has earned it the nickname of rainbird. This coucal is often encountered in riverine bush and in dense stands of grass, where it perches in low bushes and hunts for prey.

Top right

The scarletchested sunbird is one of the more striking of the six sunbird species that occur in the Park. This bird is common in rest camps, where it can be seen feeding on nectar from aloes and coral trees.

Right

Of five species of roller recorded in Kruger, only the lilac-breasted (pictured) and purple roller can be seen throughout the year. Whether hawking insects or perching on a branch near the roadside, lilacbreasted rollers display a feathery palette of dazzling colours.

Previous pages, and Opposite left

Herds of female waterbuck and their young occupy a home range that coincides with the territories of several males. Relative to their small population size, more waterbuck are killed by lion than any other antelope in Kruger, and 60 to 80 per cent of deaths can be attributed to these predators. Waterbuck are uncommon throughout their range in South Africa and currently number a modest 1 400 in Kruger. They favour open woodland near water.

Opposite right

Although kudu drink when water is available, in times of drought they are more susceptible to a lack of adequate browse than they are to a lack of drinking water. The female weighs about 160 kilograms, but males are much larger and weigh on average 250 kilograms.

Below

A nyala male displays the stripes and horn shape typical of this antelope family. Nyala occur mainly north of the Letaba River, especially along the Shingwedzi and Luvuvhu rivers. Only males have horns. Females are a reddish ochre in colour and can be confused with young kudu.

Overleaf

Early morning mist rises from the central plains below Nkumbe Mountain, as the rising sun casts its tinted rays across a fever tree. The clay soils of this region, underpinned by basalt, support large concentrations of zebra and wildebeest. The lookout at Nkumbe, 94 metres above the plain, provides one of the finest panoramas in the Park, and herds of zebra and wildebeest can often be seen trekking across the grasslands below.

Warthogs lack a thick coat of hair and have little body fat, and are therefore susceptible to cold and wet weather. Similarly, during hot summer months they are poorly protected against the scorching sun. By wallowing in mud they are able to reduce their body temperature by as much as 7°C, and mud packs also help to protect their skin from biting insects. After wallowing in mud, a convenient tree stump always serves as a rubbing post and helps locate itchy spots missed by the mud.

White rhino coat their hides in mud to reduce bites from irritating flies, and during the hot summer months mud wallows help to regulate body temperature. With a considerable body mass of up to 2 300 kilograms, and a vast surface area that is increased by folds of skin, white rhino can remove large quantities of mud from a wallow with each visit. Over the decades this has the effect of excavating significant depressions in the veld, which are rapidly filled during the rainy season to form pans.

Interesting comparisons have been drawn between the numbers of predators in Kruger and the hoofed animals on which they prey. In the Central Region, the ratio of lion to prey is 1:110, which is exceptionally high when compared to 1:1 000 in Tanzania's Serengeti. Lion (left) in Kruger sometimes change their prey preferences during wet and dry cycles. During wet cycles it is easier to stalk and catch zebra and wildebeest, while in times of drought they tend to kill more buffalo, often animals that would anyway have perished from lack of food. Most predators are small in comparison to the mass of their prey. In Kruger, the combined biomass of the major predators is equal to just one per cent of their prey species. This is because between each feeding level in the food chain there is substantial loss of energy, so a 60-kilogram hyaena (right) is dependent on 6 000 kilograms of hoofed animals, equivalent to a herd of 105 impala. The fate of all predators is therefore intricately interwoven with that of their prey.

Above

A large male leopard can weigh as much as 70 kilograms, but females are much lighter at about 30 kilograms. Impala comprise 78 per cent of the leopard's diet in Kruger. An adult leopard requires prey equivalent to about 20 impala per year, so leopard predation is not a major limiting factor on impala numbers.

Previous page left
A young baboon tests a handful of roots for palatability. Baboons are born after a gestation period of six months, and are carefully cared for by their mothers. Although other females in the troop like to play with the infant, the mother will only allow them to hold it once it has learned to walk. When an adult male is threatened by dominant males, he will often grab an infant from any female in the troop, which successfully foils the attack.

Previous page right
Young hyaena often rest outside their roadside dens. Hyaena clans are dominated by females, and a female pup inherits her mother's social status. Litters consist of one or two cubs, and if two females are born then one will invariably kill the other.

Right

The roan antelope is classified as an endangered species in South Africa. Following the harsh drought of 1992/93, roan nearly became extinct in the Park, and the population fell from 452 in 1986 to 44. Kruger mostly contains habitats that are marginal to their requirements, as roan survive better on wetter savannas. They avoid areas of short grass and overutilised areas, and occur only in open woodland with a well-developed cover of tall grass.

Giraffe browse on about 70 species of trees and shrubs in
the Kruger Park, but are particularly partial to combretums,
buffalo thorn and acacias, as illustrated above. They feed
by wrapping their long tongues around twigs to reach the
fine leaves of these trees.

Kudu are nonselective browsers and feed on no less than 150 species of trees and shrubs. They avoid trees with a high tannin content in their leaves, and favour acacia and combretum species. Although they prefer the same trees that are sought after by giraffe, competition between the two species is minimised by feeding at different heights. This beautiful large antelope is the most widely distributed of the Park's 20 antelope species, but is most common in the Central Region where its favourite food plants are found in abundance.

Previous page, and Above

In winter, buffalo concentrate (previous page) within eight kilometres of permanent water, especially along the Sabie, Olifants, Letaba and Shingwedzi rivers, and the sight of a herd of several hundred buffalo raising clouds of red dust as they trek to water is one of the most memorable that the Park can offer. A dominant buffalo bull asserts his position by holding his head high while pointing his nose towards the ground. Head-tossing and a hooking motion of the horns (above) are also used. If this fails, the bull will batter his solid horn boss against that of his rival until he gives in.

Opposite

Juvenile wild dogs playfully interact at a den site south of Lower Sabie. Fighting among pack members is rare, and a relaxed tail indicates a dog's playful mood. The pups are boisterous, and the mother disciplines them by holding them down on the ground by their necks.

Overleaf

Redbilled oxpeckers are particularly partial to giraffe. These birds consume vast numbers of ticks each day, and their loud hissing call is the sound most often associated with the usually silent giraffe.